The

Eyes

of a

Flounder

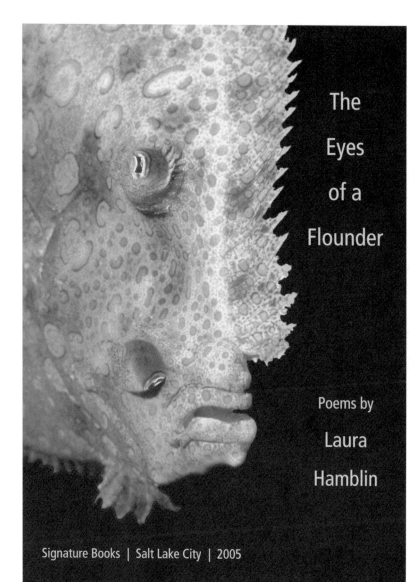

The

Eyes

of a

Flounder

Poems by

Laura

Hamblin

Signature Books | Salt Lake City | 2005

Cover and book design by Connie Disney

The Eyes of a Flounder was printed on acid-free paper
and was composed, printed, and bound in the
United States of America. © Signature Books. Signature
Books is a registered trademark of Signature Books
Publishing, LLC. All rights reserved.

10 09 08 07 06 05   6   5   4   3   2   1

www.signaturebooks.com

Library of Congress Cataloging-in-Publication Data
Hamblin, Laura.
       The eyes of a flounder : poems / by Laura Hamblin.
       p. cm.
       ISBN 1-56085-188-0 (pbk. : acid-free paper)
       I. Title.

   PS3608.A549439E96 2005
   811'.6--dc22
                                              2005051717

in memory of

J. Blake Donner

1980-2005

Acknowledgements

I gratefully acknowledge the publications in which the following poems, some in earlier versions, first appeared. *Dialogue: A Journal of Mormon Thought* published "Mormon Conversions," "The Next Weird Sister Builds a Dog Run," "How Could We Have Known," and "This Then, November"; *Exponent II*: "Celibacy at Forty-two (I)" (published as "Beyond Starlings"); *Green Fuse*: "Toward Parachute"; *Harvest: Contemporary Mormon Poems*: "The Next Weird Sister Attempts Repentance"; *Midland Review*: "To Baptize"; *Pegasus*: "For Those Who Refuse to Be Named"; *Petroglyphs*: "Cabaza de Vaca in Wal-Mart: Adventures in the Interior of America"; *Red Rocks Review*: "And the Nights" (published as "Fragment"); *River Styx*: "The Bad Mother," "The Next Weird Sister Contemplates Silicone Implants," and "The Next Weird Sister Loses Light"; *Sequel*: "Bulbs in November"; *Sophia*: "Child of Rain," "Sophia," and "Out of Necessity"; *Sunstone*: "Lament for Leah," "The Next Weird Sister Attempts Repentance," and "A Night in Snow Canyon"; and *Wisconsin Review*: "From the Next Weird Sister." Thanks also to the Utah Arts Council for awarding a shorter version of this manuscript the First Place Poetry Prize in the 2003, Forty-fifth Annual Utah Original Writing Competition.

Contents

I

On the Edge of Enclosure

II

From Being Human

III
With That Name

I

On the Edge of Enclosure

"As if departure came after the journey. As if we forever prepared to leave, knowing we could reach only the excruciating point of departure."

—Edmond Jabès
"Third Approach to the Book"

Unfinished Still Life Begun

Not a Giacometti   portrait.

   Not Stein   sitting 92 times
      while Picasso squares
her up—then
after she's gone, him
   painting her whole.

Pulsipher
      saying, "May I paint you?"
And you
laughing, "Paint
   the Tree of Knowledge!"

Upstairs
in his studio where
     the afternoon sun
        washes three walls

of window, you see where
     he and his wife make love.

     Saturdays, from three to four,
you watch him watch
          you,
    roots exposed.

He grafts your hands to

your face. Hope
in so much sun
    drops   ripe fruit.

     —magenta? cobalt? vert?

This light
   questions
   all color—all lines.

From the Next Weird Sister

It matters not that my ankles are shapely
and graceful, or that once, I remember
it well, they said I had a splendid head
of hair—perhaps the loveliest in all of Scotland.
One need not be a beldam to be
a witch. It takes only a desperate, malignant

need to which there can be no
relinquishment. Be saucy and over-bold.
Your charms enough will change you.
For now the sun is setting, and our clan meets
again. Here on the heath we spread the spoils
of our battle and offer them to vacant

sable skies. The fair men have called foul
fair. And the foul men have called fair
foul. The fog is lifting, but the filth in the air remains.
Sometimes I wish I were a birth-strangled babe.
Then at least my finger would have a price. And I
might be understood or might understand the unknown

powers. But I was destined to live
and am driven to accomplish deeds without names.
Sisters, come away. When labor is
too great—then is when a birth occurs.
I, mother of maggots, I lay the eggs of my brain
in night visions; there to incubate, molt and corrode,

there to pardon and poison all entrails.
And what of you? It matters not that your neck
is slender—or you, that your breasts are warm and firm.
You, with that raging void—you too can be
a midnight hag. It occurs to us all, at one time
or another, when a broken heart is the gift
and the wound, sin can be a soothing salve.

Toward Parachute

Going west, filling what
we assume is empty
space, we count, dead,
on this side only
of the divided highway,
forty-eight deer.
They might have moved
as solid as will
under a ringed moon,
through mad migration,
while the nights were
still long for three
days more, not seeing
the repeated road signs
—black deer leaping
through diamonds, yellow.
Soon those with antlers
sprout leaves, take root.
Next spring they shed seeds
like cottonwood. Next
winter their shameless
progeny strip bark,
move through their thin
instinct in the direction
of hunger. Years from
now we return, plant
alfalfa, open an Amoco—
give directions, if asked.
But now, to the syllables
of melting snow with
this specific odor
of stillness, we drive
toward some sort
of consequence, counting.

October First

Far-off slate of our eyes

      see the maples' red
      scream—scream something

like the high wall of death—

      as common as paradox,
      as odd as love, when

black air snaps with cold.

      Say this is the height,
      the depth of harvest. Here,

where the geese rise and depart,

      moving with them, like us,
      their own boarder—

the sharp wedge of winter. Here,

      where the moon looms large,
      larger than we can remember.

Out of Necessity

When Nietzsche, practiced
voyeur—estranged and
syphilitic—saw the emaciated
horse beaten, the man

who said "god is dead"
beat the one who whipped, broke
the whip in rage, knelt before
the horse, as if one could

breathe too much, and wept.
With pity he tried, willed
with the weight of the maker,
to enlarge the void

in his arms, to hold
the beast, tried to comfort
the animal, dead as when
Mary held god dead, and wept.

The Next Weird Sister Loses Light

In our house there is more than one bedroom.
Chaste, we insist we are chaste, and yet we
grope on hands and knees for what will illume,
while corners increase exponentially.
These nights no one makes a cry. There is no
trimming. The moon goes out. Fences barb our
house. We can find no door, no exit, though
the mastiffs' mouths enlarge while they devour
our oily sins again. Darkly we call
to footsteps we can hear are out of sight.
"Are you a groom?" At night's middle a small
blackness answers, "There are only *ifs*." All
of us rise and stagger to make aright
our lamps. So blinded but for oil, we fall.

My Hate

My hate curls through coral:
a moray's mouth, open.
When something moves,
it lurches.
It doesn't ask,
"Plant? Animal? Mineral?"
It swallows everything,
whole. Love yells
from the fence top—
a balancing
tight-rope act.
My hate peers
from under the porch—
looks through lattice,
sees with pupils dilated,
sees things squared—
is focused. Hate knows.
Love is mutable:
scales of a trout
flashing in the sun.
My hate is constant:
mud at the bottom.
It can't be dredged.
The buildup of debris,
stuck under pressure.
My hate is a wall.
I lean against it.
My hate says,
"This thing I won,"
says, "This thing I earned."
It fits; it fevers,
is familiar. My hate
cannot be removed.
It is too close
to the thing I hate:
a gasping breath, suffocation.
My hate waits
behind shower curtains.

When I least expect it,
it pours itself over:
ice-water shocking,
heart-stopping cold.
Love says, "Why not?"
My hate says, "Why?"
says, "Prove it!" says,
"Get lost!"
My hate is for keeps.
It's there, like
thick oil on water,
undrinkable.
Love naps in
the afternoon sun,
sleeps in late,
doesn't set the clock.
My hate is the ax
that breaks the glass.
A screaming alarm—
Class dismissed!
My hate is the taste
of my own blood
cut on the edge,
swallowed, waiting
for the sign
I've consumed it:
coffee-ground vomit,
shit full of bile.
My hate I keep
in a shoe box, buried
in the back yard
under a tree. At night
it moans and sings
dirges—dares me to
dig it up, stares
me down with sockets
of its once
obsidian eyes.

To Seed

In the back, next
        to the wall   where
scales of cream paint
strip,   someone did not

tend the garden. Here
morning   glories open
their   pink knowledge
to the bright,   glinting

sun, glister and
twine   in a silent   whine
    round the pulpy
stocks of last year's

onions, whose   tuberous
arms   raise   the   white
    flags of surrender, three
feet into the grainy light.

Their   sepals and pistils
sheen   a raucous   blue.
Here, someone   can
afford

to   wait. Herby and
germinal,   the garden
    pullulates, luxuriates, buds,
sprouts and   burgeons.

Here, someone can present
these
    arguments   of gain;
someone
    can come
      to her senses.

The Bad Mother

The bad mother gains employment
with AT&T. Her tools hang from her belt,
clank like clappers from a cracked bell.
She climbs the telephone pole, digging
in her boot spikes as deep and sure
as any accusing look. The bad mother
cuts the wires, holds one end to her ear,
holds the other across her heart and up
against her lips, keeps herself still.
The starlings take no notice. They line up
on the wires, along her shoulders, over
the top of her head. The bad mother holds
her breath. The stars keep shining.
She hears the good mothers repeat
their polite dreams. She hears the good
children say "Thank you" and "Please"
and "Don't worry." The bad mother
shrinks like a dry sponge. Clematis grow
up the pole, through her legs, around her
back. The blossoms opening in the spring
and dropping in the fall are the bad mother's
eyes slowly blinking. The bad
mother waits for the child's voice;
her hands grasp the wire like some steel
umbilical cord. She waits for the
voice she would recognize anywhere—
the voice that grew inside her
before there was anything to say,
the voice next to the pinpoint eyes waiting
for light in the perfect black, the voice
suffocated in two tiny blue lungs—
with no possible notion of air.

Mormon Conversions

The songs mutate
like a virus in my blood:
"I Am a Child
of God," "Firm as the Mountains
around Us," "The Golden Plates."
I am twelve, have spent
twelve years learning
my insufficiencies,

my inabilities.
I will never spread
the white table cloth, never
break bread or fill
the tiny cups
with water, never
speak sacred words over
them, pass them.

Under the bright even
sky, boys with shellacked
faces play basketball.
Closer to god (in the next
life with numerous
wives), they know power,
vertical like the Mount
of Zion, and wide—

I begin to bleed,
am taught with the other
girls to crochet, to knit
a pattern of life,
a pair of slippers
for our fathers.
Ah, dark skein—
unraveling girl.

Now, on the rock our fathers
planted, in this house
of love, making
covenants, the congregation
stands. We sing, "The Spirit
of God Like a Fire
Is Burning," and the live
coal of reality ignites.

Bulbs in November

When the wind-
fall apples are
dusty brown
and the wind,
like a wave, lifts
leaves parched
and thin—reach deep
into the bucket where
the bulbs have
lingered half
the month long;
touch the dark
humus, open a small
hollow; place
the bulbs, thick
laughing buddhas,
their arms raised
still, into the chill
rank dirt; finger
the dimensions of
the moment—wait in
the capacious silence,
conspicuous
as always, until
swallows rise
like sparks,
like the ring of glass
through the heavy
fragment of snow.

On Being Stopped in Traffic by a Water Buffalo
—Hyderabad, India, July 1, 2003

This one creature, slate
grey-blue as Krishna,
could make you
(when the sky descends,
rain-dragged, and yokes
itself to earth), could
make you believe. This
one creature, hide hard
as if tanned in his own
skin, could make you bound
to the world (to the degree
you know that fierce
knot—tying lover
to beloved—of knowledge)
and know you'll be
back for more: again
and more, and you'll never
get over your own
life. This one
creature makes you hope
(hope—the last of long
lists at the tattered
periphery of desire),
hope gopis *did* dance
in raga adoration
'round their ghee-
faced god—as now
the egrets following
like devotees, praising
this one creature
through component
notes (in the semi-
permeable light), picking
parasites off the thin
bone of the back—

this one back, bending
under the weight
of your patience, the
gaze of the world—
ready to die, flaming
(always and at last)
as the charred spoke
of the wheel
of desire turns
and turns—and burns.

Child of Rain

Head bent, half
looking up. Shy
eye turned sky-
ward. It is for
you, this shattered
water, as you wander,
as you wade inside
each infant drop
until, like your
wet loss, you are
both quenched
and swallowed.

Celibacy at Forty-two
(I)

Dawn is release
from another night
single while black birds
gather in the fields
and eat and chatter
of better meals and worse.
And single, I listen.
Away—beyond black birds,
beyond fields—
I am soothed by a sound
of cars in dim light:
the sound of people
going somewhere,
or of people who have been.

The Next Weird Sister Builds a Dog Run

With fortune's damned,
    quarreling smile,
        the neighbors complain

as they do with each move.
    She snarls and follows bloody
        instructions, measuring off

a corner of cruelty,
    figuring, in metrical codes,
        the division of her loves,

her errors. Her dogs
    pace the length of chain
        link, jump with

vaulting ambition,
    snap at the crossed
        purpose of penning.

Dog nights she stands
    on the edge of enclosure
        and listens

to nasal whines
    while the disciples of
        lies call her

to this sacrilege.
    Here laws cease to
        operate. With the opposite

of faith she submits
    to this new religion.
        Still, through locked gates,

she pets dull fur,
        whispers pet names,
                serves each mouth red milk.

Neighbors console themselves
        in steel and wire dreams. As if a run
                will hold dogged thoughts.

She knows better and moves
        out a straw mat, if not
                to sleep, then

to lie with obsession,
        comforting some poor dog
                a hundred choices ago.

II
From Being Human

"Wasn't love and departure
placed so gently on shoulders that it seemed to be made
of a different substance than in our world?"

—Rainier Maria Rilke
"The Second Duino Elegy"

Letter to No One in Particular

Morning always comes too early—the sun
a pale wafer of light, offered at the
alter of dawn. Bland yellow yarrow
stiffens slowly. On this October day
I first notice my visible breath and
think how loss pulls language from us until
we wander through a gallery of words,
until we fill this fibrous space. The
future is a pocket, a dark empty
hole, contained and containing;
my hand enters and curls softly
on itself.

          We hardly see the thin
line that divides possession and loss;
we think such lines are to be colored
within or outside of—that such is
the nature of art. Someone should say:
the line dividing possession and loss
is the line we draw *with*.

                    I almost live
alone. Three dogs inhabit my house and
move through it like dark angels. The cat
sleeps on the sewing basket; the raspy hum
of the sewing machine answers his soft
purr. On the table lies a bowl full of
apples—a gift left from Cézanne. If
I were to touch them, my finger would
turn red.

          But now the room is without flat
surfaces, allowing the hours to stretch
and curve, and makes me think of form—
form, which always answers to emptiness.
Words, gentle and humble, blow like leaves
across my doorway. They speak of what I
would, when next I say my say. They pause
for a moment; at their leaving, I speak.
Isn't it absence—remorseless in its

presence—which moves me
to the foreground of my life? Isn't it
the clarity of night which reminds
me I have always lived in a house
which is not my house—in this square
mile of my solitude? And isn't it
desire which returns me again to
this common supply of matter?
The story of poetry is the
story of all the doors I have failed
to open, saying, "you may enter by
invitation, but by invitation
only."

    And now, for an hour more
the stars will quilt the sky. I write this
letter to no one in particular—
all the while expecting no answer.

When We Fell

When we fell
apart after
yesterday's love-
making, the smell
of rain still
in the air, I knew
it was our last as
you washed
my thigh, purposefully
and without smiling.
Not like a lover, but
like the surgeon
you are, as if
carefully closing
a wound.

A Night in Snow Canyon

This is the place
of inverted
valleys, where black
magma and red
sandstone meet.

Lie in the dry
river bed. Wait
for sleep. Listen
to the footsteps
of motionless pilgrims.

There is your parent and
your child—murmuring
of things that were,
speechless of things
that will be.

Bats with familiar
faces fly through
the night, guided
only by echoes
of themselves.

Wind moves over
your body like the airy
fingers of a lost
lover: a warm
pressure, here—then not

here. Stars spin in their space-
worn orbits forever
defining north, as if
eternity had anything

to do with time.

In My Pregnant Dream

Swallows stop building nests.
Salmon no longer swim upstream.
There are children, children
everywhere. They have been born,
and continue to be born. Children
who never came to me
because of pills, abstinence,
no love to make. They crowd
me, sucking my air, myself. My
pregnant sister sits in her
chair. She lifts her shirt
to show her capacious self.
Her skin stretches, red veins
on transparent flesh. But the growth
inside of her is no true
baby, only a bloated blue head,
half the skull caved in and
decayed. It turns and looks
at me—its eyes do not
blink. Its lips move. Blood
flows, turning from red to brown.

The Next Weird Sister Contemplates Silicone Implants

In this thin
place I wait, seven
cells deep, while
the reality of living
in skin is known—
liver spots and
carbuncles. I
turn sideways to
the mirror, encounter
and count: two withered
paps, dry vaulted
hollows, this flat seat
of love. What haven't I
done to draw men's
eyes? Padded layers
of thick lingerie. Pinned
rolled socks to the edge
of these wrinkles.
Sealed with cement great
mounds of money—cold
coins, folded
bills against this
sternum. Hopeless
chests hold little.
What's to be
done with this
concavity but turn
the blades of knives
inward and implant that
which will make me
more mammal? Then
wait, with desire, with
the constant desire
to be someone else,
to be inside of someone
else, or have someone
inside of me.

To Baptize

They want to baptize my son,
take his slight body,
immerse him in the wetness
of water, make him stainless,
wash from him sins
he did not commit, sins
that belong to no one.
They want to stand him
in the water, have him
shudder and pimple,
soak his paleness
in a pool of solvent,
dilute him into a true person,
bleach him to the dry
white of dead sailor's bones.
They want to bend him
backwards—nose, eyes closed,
fist holding wrist,
bend him back as the moon
bends the tide, then
pulls it forth again.
They want to cover him
completely, hold him under till
he knows deep, Atlantic loneliness,
while he waits for the pull
of human mercy to save him
from being human, the faith
of dry men allowing him
terrible air again,
to bring him forth as something new,
as if there were shades of white,
as if he weren't already water-born.

Heisenberg in Baja

The dunes drift southward to the rush of wave.
The sun, an orange piñata, bursts and flings
a spray of golden light upon each crest.
He walks the shifting line of continent
content, until his hand full open
touches on a shell, and he recalls all
those years ago, his wife, how—in her youth
her hands and eyes could throw a wild fiesta
by themselves—her white fingers thin and splayed
placed the rubber bands on the door knob.
He watched her, and he thought of seeing
(as if we witness this frail world and can
remain an innocent—as if it were
science, and not desire that gives us faith,
and makes us all believers of a sort).
He watched, and when she was aware he watched,
she bent her head and tucked a wisp of hair
behind her ear. Her eyes, a mute gray-blue,
seemed to say "Don't. Don't look at me that way."

Celibacy at Forty-two
(II)

Nights I make
a nest—flannel and foam,
invite all the small
things: two dogs and a cat,
a slick gray mouse,
even the plump
spider, its abdomen
pearl-round and white.
I open the windows
as wide as my loss
until all the small birds
find their way.
Juncos root at the foot
of my bed. Nighthawks dive
through the dark. My own
blue breath beds down
with the slight air at my neck,
with the dark curl of
my knees. And all
night long, I'm never
alone, and when I awake,
there's that moment—in
the liminal blue-black space—
when for that slight slant
of time, the purr at my back is
love. But it's only
a moment—then
the chink of sun cracks,
and the hole of the day spreads
before me, and before it,
I rise. And I enter.

The Next Weird Sister Attempts Repentance

Thinking it had been a while
since she had felt
god's grace, (one should
feel sorry, loving
one's own end)—
she thought she felt
sorry, bowed her
head, opened locks
for the air, made a hell-
broth. (Can done be
undone?) She thought
she felt sorry for
the seeds of all
things yet uncreated
(He knows
thy thoughts),
for a child with a tree
in his hands (Who can
impress the forest?),
for where she had never
been about, about—wayward
(Show the grief
his heart). Thinking
heaven is murky,
she thought she felt
god's grace: Give
me . . . Give me
. . . then thought
of killing swine.

This Then, November

When the arduous season comes again,
unexpectedly, air rushes through
needled trees, causing a sudden
shift of time, a shift of light:
this new hue, this new sound.
And we listen to leaves, like words,
scratch and crack through the frigid sky
and watch as nature begins

to die—gracefully—full of our own
death. It is what we cannot pronounce,
the commonness, the thinness of our
transient present. It is with us
still, flattened, like pressed leaves:
imperishable things imagined.

Red-tailed Outside Scipio

On a seared cedar
post the red-
tailed hawk lights

still as the seventh
day, still but
for the black tack

of its singular eye,
alive and focused as sin.
With a quick bob

and a down-
slurred cry she
rises on a riot

of air—high up—
up through the gyre,
circling far above all,

calm and silent circling:
there—up there, in the blue
of the nave of the poem.

On the Advantage of Being Supine

The vertical will never know the nights,
moon-long and summered.
The nights you will lie whole
flat against your back,
the cord never so sheltered,
face upward and opened.
You will lie still, like moss
on the underside of stone,
variable and sure, and you will practice
grace. You will close your eyes
and wonder at the color of your lids,
the dark base of light.
You will know the impossibility
of cataloguing sins supine.
For while supine, when you bend your knees,
your body will become a cup for love,
the very shape of love,
the attitude and posture of slow mercy.

And the Nights

Like vestigial wings, the blades
of your sad shoulders return me to
the seamless nights, and the nights
full of light, full of silence—
that thin, monotonous harp. I fold
the chairs and the words, lean them
against the wall in the hall
now so familiar I might know
the carpet's every fiber, know history—
the time it takes for honesty.

Lament for Leah

On the night when Jacob took Leah,
when he supposed he held his love
seven years earned,
as he undid her hair,
did Leah's breath stop,
her lips holding the secret
waiting to be given away?
Did she whisper, "My love,"
as if speaking the words
would make him so?
And did Jacob wonder
at her ordinary thighs,
or did he, in his drunkenness,
grant them another's beauty?
Did Leah dare to embrace her husband
in their one essential deed,
or did she simply endure
the staining of the bed
while the soul of red opened her?
Was the morning stone-gray and still,
when the softness of sleep
left Jacob's eyes,
and he saw with revulsion
his tender-eyed wife?
Did her pride grow small
and her hopes world-narrow
as he cried out against
their sacrilege of love?
As he cried out for Rachel,
did his wife turn to prayer
for an open womb, that heart-balm
gift? Did she have any vision
of the women to come,
who will never sit near any
well's mouth, the elder sisters, given in
haste who—with fair eyes or not—
will see though the prism of marriage,
through the cut-glass prism of marriage?

Some Faith

I

During the fourth watch
(how tired he must have been
being master), walking
as one used to walking
through the near-spent night,
walking as one light,
he walked on liquid ground.
And when the twelve saw,
they were full of wonder.
They called him.
Peter was sure he said
walk with me. But the water
distorted the words.
What he really said
was talk with me.

II

Five thousand souls like
five thousand sins, original
and all the same,
rest on Galilee's cold floor;
watch above them
the strange human feet
sink in their every step:
the accumulated past—
a lake full of those
sentenced with cement
(the would-bes and derelict
saints) now dividing
themselves—fish
food, swaying like sound
over water—the multitudes
who could walk on
almost anything.

The Next Weird Sister Wonders

If a man were to come
into my house tonight,
would he hear the dim
light's dead-mineral hum—
would he feel freeway madness
in the stillness of clocks—
would he mothball my linens,
recognize a woman's
dreams, painted in water,
nailed to wood?

In the River Ouse

Say the sky is
        as bright as tin when
she lifts and counts
        the stones, placing
them in her pockets
        like solid truths
—round and hard
        and smooth.
Say that she looks
        with a dull gaze
at the Ouse's surface
        and can no longer
see her own
        reflection, just the pure,
cold stones
        on the bottom.
Say that she wades
        with breathy abruptness
into the deep wetness,
        her face as blank
as hope, the raw
        weeds leaning
toward her and quivering
        with a thin cry.
Say, as she immerses
        herself, the horizon opens—
seamlessly—and she looks
        up and sees, last
of all, that final
        syllable close.

Above It All

Fifty-two steps up
on some ranger's wet-
dream of one big
Erector set non-stop
wind wail SSW.
Fifty-two feet high I see
no smoke (big or little)
screen in sight, which
mainly means no
tree the ranger can douse
today so he can chain
saw tomorrow. Gray
jay screams lodged in
lodge pole pine 70
feet high. Sky chevy chrome
bright, five vultures (old
bald men, wrinkled pink
pin heads) circling and
half-circling now for half
an hour. Something big
must (have) die(d). Gray
jay screams—lets those five
buzzards know: baby, don't
mess with me. That same
whine wind, that same no
wan wind-oh—screen screech,
That same same shutter
stutter—same creak and crack
of 50-year-old stairs ash
gray. Gray jay (buzzards dive
south slope—some-
thing big—fat hearts
flattened under sky and
for now above earth, but
not my heart, grind pine
pain), pine green—screams
high scale frail—but
not my heart.

III
With That Name

"I know only the skin of the earth
And I know it is without a name."

—Pablo Neruda
"Too Many Names"

Between the Space

We thought that it would soon evaporate
the drops that rust the face of our routine.
A challenge and a boldness come too late,

can modify what we anticipate
(the easy, empty space we hadn't seen)—
we thought that. It would soon evaporate

as the rays of the sun accelerate.
The process and the air takes on a sheen:
a challenge and a boldness come too late.

Then all the colors change—the blues lose weight,
reds scab to brown, leaves fall from evergreen.
We thought that it would soon evaporate.

For smallness will itself rejuvenate
between the space, and in the space between
a challenge and a boldness come too late.

The lack of space cannot substantiate
the loss of what we love. I do not mean
we thought that. It would soon evaporate:
a challenge and a boldness come too late.

Le Main de Dieu

Perhaps there was no intention
to abolish the privilege
of hierarchy, yet to move
in the direction of the idea *was*
to deviate: not complete,
as anatomy describes,
but as unfinished form,
a hand rising from stone, holding
a stone in which emerge two
figures, curled and partial
as if in a womb, movement
in stone, with a line starting
from the brain, form from matter
like the first shy breath celebrating
shadow, a volume living in
space, creating its own
space, filling all the chambers

of the heart, containing everything
in a triangle or a cube so that
the small fingers, as whole as the
large, clasp their mate's head or
hold a reflection of their own
freedom: duration and becoming—
Adam creating god creating Adam.

How Could We Have Known

that loneliness is like
the whole of the moon
rising in a sky so lucent,
the clouds cast shadows
and make the night
suddenly aware of darkness;

that loneliness is the comfort only
a drowning man feels when his body
repents of its image of god,
when his lungs cry out darkly: don't
leave me, don't leave me behind,
but the drowning man drowns alone;

that loneliness is balanced
on a line stretching fine and thin,
the darkened one which holds all things
angled, axled, and endlessly spinning,
defining this odd symmetry,
this abbreviated gift of flesh.

Cabeza de Vaca in Wal-Mart: Adventures in the Interior of America

I

Not by conduct
but by accident:
a touted pilot,
a ship lodged in some tree-
tops, keels scraping bottom;
the days we stood stranded,
unbalanced men
embarking and tempting god,
destitute of means
either to remain or to leave.
The loss of everything
we had—not much,
but valuable to us.

II

Prevailed upon—discouraging,
the country our sin had cast us in,
uncharted. Obedience
to credit is the one
superstition of these people.
All are ignorant of time. They do
not reckon by the sun, moon,
month or year; they understand
the seasons in terms of Hallmark
cards and holiday decorations,
in which dating they are well adept:
Any time and every time,
slashed prices,
the beginning and the end
of sales.

III

Wilderness.
In effort to survive,
regaining senses, locomotion, hope,
inundated with convenient locations
and service hours:
fine hose, fiddle faddle,
empty kiddie pools, juice
extractors, condoms and condiments,
we went into the interior as far
as we dared, then prevailed
upon the natives to receive us
as slaves, finding the interior more
populous and more amply provisioned
(Not available in Broward County, FL).

IV

Whence come ye, and
what may be your merchandise?
To sojourn to the end
of fluorescent lights,
the unknown reaches, wildness.
Strangers vied in approbation,
exhibiting credentials
of their dogged quest of goods.
We sallied.
Had we been prepared,
we still could not have known
where to go—reduced
again, to the last extremity.
The saddest thing in America:
to have nothing
to buy, to have
nothing to sell.

V

Through the two thousand
leagues, sojourning
eight years we were presented
with a certificate
of the day, month, year,
items purchased, and price
paid. American letters:
concerned with ultimates,
shaped by exigencies
of a new and strange
environment (peculiarly
American)—the journey is our
home, we end in
citizenship forged
in the trials of abundance.

In a Field in Todos Santos

Even here, where
our language is not
spoken, in the evening
often you rise
and skirt low across
the field—a nighthawk,
your wings banded;
even here, glazing
over the blue
blanket of dusk,
you pass through our
past and into
my present, accompanied
by the insects' dry
drone, their cadence
distended, whom
you consume,
even as they sing.

For the Love of Shams

Rumi gave his body
over to its own
trembling, to its
every sob. He chose
to reside in bright
darkness, to pitch
his tent in extravagant
flames. He spun
until the world
itself stood still and
silent and whole.
Fallen, how the world
sustained him, until
Shams surrendered
to the present,
and every detail
of the earth—cracked
cups, reeded
flutes, undyed silk—
was sanctified,
and he danced
the wheeling dance
that is called prayer.

Twenty-three Miles South of Canada

Here there must be a thousand shades
of green: bleary, tentative, enameled,
and beyond that, blue-greens—
fragile and melancholy. Here
you thrive on thinness: thin air,
thin coffee, thin socks. Here you can
forget the softness of tolerance
and the eight sharp corners
of compromise. Here the long clouds
stretch over the arch of
sky and the deep clouds rise, form
anvils and fall. Night heavy, muttering rain
opens thick layers of silence which cradle
the slim new moon. Here shrieks
of long-necked birds flatten
in the white summer heat, in the
arrow shafts of light. Language
itself breaks apart—a flotilla
of words riding waves. With
the break and the bend of morning
you carefully make a list of things
you can do without; you recite the
list like a prayer. You discover
vertical sensitivity: rock, tree, cloud.
You say the words again and again:
rock, tree, cloud—until language is
reduced to thought, thought
to image, image to shadow,
shadow to light. Until already
it feels like another country.

The Next Weird Sister Loses Weight

I binge on
fried chicken,
on chocolate
and pig fat,
but to no
gain.
There is
less of me
lately—
a shrinking
from east
to west,
a reduction
of mass
and density.
Without
even trying,
I have
diminished
into moth-
paleness,
ambiguous
and spare
as a shadow
in a slat.
There is a
tenuous
decrease:
rib chested,
knobby spined,
I ossify.
I know
the shortest
distance
between two
points. Only
the space
between the

atoms expands.
I could
hold parties
in the vacancy,
invite
beetles and
toads to
twirl in
wild, calorific
dances, two-
dimensional
in the neck
of my collar,
in the hand
of my cuff.
I have
become only
the drop-
echo of
myself.
Reduced . . .
reduced . . .
I wonder, if
I were all
here, would
the earth
have more
pull on me?
Lean, empty,
I wander
spindle-legged
through narrow
columns,
searching.
Where did
I go? Where
did I go?

The Difference between
Loneliness and Solitude

I

At the doorway, listening
to the call of the unnamed birds,
nerve-riddles—an affront,
reminding you of
how little you know

Listening, between the palm leaves
you hear the cactus wrens'
call and answer—the laughing
a caw and joke—a joke in which
you are included

II

Like undiagnosed cancer,
like at the police station
waiting to be picked up, or the time
you need to knit a sweater
without needle or yarn

Slow, like Saturday morning coffee,
or like tomatoes ripening on the vine,
when all the lights of night
circling the North Star—
all ancient and bright

III

Huge, like the Atlantic,
where the horizon rises up
to the sky but never touches:
an emptiness fathered
through deprivation

Like the Pacific, large,
lacing will and desire
measureless and lucid:
an expanse whose mother
is abundance

Dog Star

Panting at Orion's heel with an eye out
for Lepus. At your helical setting,
farmers sow beans, lucern, millet;
at your rising, you flood
the Nile. Luminous and serious,
heralding sunrise to the east,
light becomes visible when you set.
In and out of the Milky Way,
your baleful barking dries
up the body. Canicular days, you bicker
in a stellar blue and white.
Scorning, tremulous wave
of light, we cut the heart of a fawn-
colored dog at your festival three
times a year—to ensure the blossom
of fruit, to avert mildew and rust,
to hallow our fat harvest. What
others mistake for a silent sky
is the trough of the wave of your howl.

The Lover Freed

When the Beloved whistled the thin icy notes,
the Lover freed the impounded dogs,
each with a rhinestone collar.
When the Beloved walked the dogs,
the Lover howled verbs at the moon,
conjunctions dropped like falling stars.
When the Beloved begged for silence,
the Lover unstrung the harps
and used the strings for fishing line.
When the Beloved filleted the salmon,
the Lover painted the barbecue red,
spilling paint throughout the yard.
When the Beloved mowed the lawn,
the Lover mosaiced a birdbath
with porcelain blue wedding plates.
When the Beloved identified all the birds,
the Lover wrote with a leaky pen
the names of the birds in every book.
When the Beloved hung out the laundry,
the Lover set out seven pails,
catching each wet crystal drop.
When the Beloved froze the water,
the Lover took an ice pick
and chiseled a thin piccolo.
When the Beloved whistled the thin icy notes,
the Lover freed the impounded dogs,
each with a rhinestone collar.

Riftia

Eight thousand feet down
in the blue-black of pressure

on the ocean's rifted floor—
they twist. With no morphology,

independent for millennia
of nouns and pronouns,

manifold tubes—eight feet of worm,
outside of reason, outside of

time—proliferate whitely:
less eye, less mouth, less heart.

Of all unembraceable life
this world holds, they alone

have no need for the sun.
With the patience of fossils,

for us these lovers have waited.
When we look in the blank

that must be faced,
appellative whispers rise on the waves,

sing through the miles of cold heresy.
"Adam, O Adam," they call and they call—

"What name do you give to us, Adam?"

Eating Lies

Ls leak from your lip, drip, thick syrup, through the hairs of your chest, round over your stomach. . . . When they reach your thigh—I lick them up. Capital Os, pasty and swollen, burst from your mouth and rise like soft dough. Inside my hard throat they are kneaded. Lower case ws tip from the space between your teeth, free fall, twist into ms, break with icy cracks into small mal-formed vs—vs that I swallow, point first. I scuttle on hands and knees after es as they clank on the floor, as they catch with each roll. Full of dark vowels, I gather the small, inarticulate sounds—a comma, a dash, that pitiful pause, the diphthong's quick, slick slide. O legion, legion, father of lies, fill with noise this hole-y night. Whatever you offer I take, suck, and chew. When a small y catches, I retch—What comes up is indecipher-able: qs without tails, crosses of ts, the autonomous dot of an i.

The Next Weird Sister Has a Yard Sale

Take the tailless rat, backbone
twitching, white breath unthawed.
Or here—this insane root, blind
and growing in the cellar's sucking dark.
Have the old broken things:
the Tartar's skinny lips,
the Jew's bracketed liver,
this hateful girdle curving
the corner of my hip. I sell
the familiar pets: brindle cat,
systolic snake, the braided
hairs of my chin, mother's
thick yellow nails, crescent clippings
in these too blue jars. Hedge-pig's grunt,
this bat's wool, the pilot's arching thumb
—for you, a dollar and a quarter.
Everything ordinary, useful,
stuck or visible goes—
I've no need for it all:
excess, bric-a-brac, empty maws!
I keep only your T-shirt, red
and smelling of sex, and a fat stick
of lime. When night breaks,
I draw a circle 'round my scabby self—
so small it keeps out everything
but this: the knowing and the not knowing.

Celibacy at Forty-two
(III)

what is love like
love is like the eyes of a flounder
grown on one side of its head

what is the night like
the night is like my long arms,
my long fingers

what are you afraid of
I am afraid of baby
bats hanging upside down

what is the saddest thing you know
a political prisoner in China lived
40 years in solitary confinement

what do you miss
I miss good lies, keeping
time by another's breath, guilt

what is the softest thing you have touched
the long nose of a horse,
the small concave between crossed legs

what will you wear tomorrow
tomorrow I will wear the touch of a masseur,
a gray scarf, the stain of pomegranates

where have you been
inside of magenta,
outside of enough

what did you forget
I forgot to have a daughter
I forgot to have a daughter

what do you love
I love orange lichen, getting
the second line, silence flowing back in

where do you live
I live in a marsh wren's nest
in a room made of poetry

how do you decorate
I decorate in silence,
in gauze and red beads

what do you celebrate
the smell of coffee, the inside of my
mouth, shampooing with a bucket of rain

what will you give back
I will give back two silver earrings,
enough covers, my insecurity

what is so difficult
differential equations, a habit
of closure, returning to the body

For Those Who Refuse to Be Named

to sit one morning sideways
on a kitchen chair,
hair uncombed, head
bent, a bowl of fruit
in the crease of her leg

or on a balcony, reading,
unconscious of her
fingers at her mouth
before she turns the next page,
while the round sun grows white—

there is no one here with that name

Sophia

When the bread molds,
Sophia will come, wandering
under a leprous moon.

We will erase the open books,
the crowded margins,
when Sophia comes.

When Sophia comes,
she will tame Palamabron's
mad horses—and nothing will change.

She will come with her
ten thousand infants,
each of them cut in two.

And when Sophia comes,
I will comb her gray hair,
hold her thin head to my chest.

She will ask my forgiveness,
singing the song she teaches,
in a language I never heard,

in a language I never knew.

Notes

Cabeza de Vacathe	The first European to walk across the continent of North America (taking eight years to do so) after his ship wrecked off the coast of Florida in 1527.
Heisenberg, Werner Karl	German physicist (1901-76) whose uncertainty principle became the cornerstone of quantum mechanics.
Le Main de Dieu	Title of a sculpture by Auguste Rodin.
Palamabron	Symbolizes the poet's pity for the opressed.
Parachute	Small southwestern Colorado town on Interstate 70.
Riftia	Tube worms which reside in a symbiotic relationtionship with sulfuric bacteria near hydrothermal vents on the ocean floor.
River Ouse	River in Yorkshire, England, where the novelist Virginia Woolf drowned herself in 1941.
Scipio	Small town in south-central Utah.
Shams of Tabriz	Companion and mystical friend of Jelaluddin Rumi, the thirteenth-century Farsi poet who founded the Mevlevi order of Dervishes, also known as the whirling Dervishes of Sufism.
Snow Canyon	State park in southwestern Utah outside the town of St. George.
Todos Santos	Small village in Southern Baja California, Mexico.

Laura Hamblin is a professor of English at Utah Valley State College, where she received the 2002 Faculty Excellence Award. She also received the 1997 Eisteddfod Crown for Poetry from Brigham Young University and First Place Award in 2003 in the Utah Original Writing Competition. Her poems have been published in *Green Fuse*, *Pegasus*, *Petroglyph*, *River Styx*, *Sequel*, *Red Rock Review*, *Sunstone*, *Wisconsin Review*, and elsewhere, and her critical essays have appeared in *A Companion to Jane Austen Studies* and *Natural History*, among others. In 2003 she participated in an International Education Exchange to Hyderabad, India. She lives in Hobble Creek Canyon east of Utah Valley.